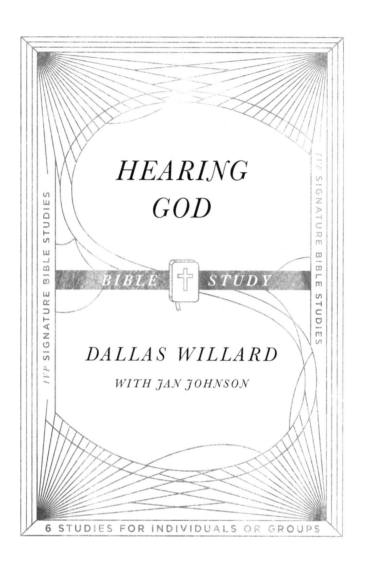

HEARING GOD

BIBLE ✝ STUDY

DALLAS WILLARD

WITH JAN JOHNSON

6 STUDIES FOR INDIVIDUALS OR GROUPS

An imprint of InterVarsity Press
Downers Grove, Illinois

InterVarsity Press
P.O. Box 1400, Downers Grove, IL 60515-1426
ivpress.com
email@ivpress.com

This study guide is based on and adapts material from Hearing God © *1984, 1993, 1999, 2012 by Dallas Willard.*

InterVarsity Press® is the book-publishing division of InterVarsity Christian Fellowship/USA®, a movement of students and faculty active on campus at hundreds of universities, colleges, and schools of nursing in the United States of America, and a member movement of the International Fellowship of Evangelical Students. For information about local and regional activities, visit intervarsity.org.

Cover design and image composite: David Fassett
Interior design: Daniel van Loon
Image: field and mountains: © James O'Neil / The Image Bank / Getty Images

ISBN 978-0-8308-4847-8 (print)
ISBN 978-0-8308-4848-5 (digital)

Printed in the United States of America ∞

InterVarsity Press is committed to ecological stewardship and to the conservation of natural resources in all our operations. This book was printed using sustainably sourced paper.

Library of Congress Cataloging-in-Publication Data

Names: Willard, Dallas, 1935-2013. author. | Johnson, Jan, 1952- author.

Title: Hearing God Bible study : 6 studies for individuals or groups /
    Dallas Willard with Jan Johnson.

Description: Downers Grove, IL : InterVarsity Press, [2021] | Series: IVP
    signature Bible studies | Includes bibliographical references.

Identifiers: LCCN 2021034701 (print) | LCCN 2021034702 (ebook) | ISBN
    9780830848478 (paperback) | ISBN 9780830848485 (ebook)

Subjects: LCSH: Willard, Dallas, 1935-2013. In search of guidance. |
    Spiritual life—Christianity—Textbooks. | God
    (Christianity)—Will—Textbooks.

Classification: LCC BV4501.3 .W54393 2021 (print) | LCC BV4501.3 (ebook)
    | DDC 248.4—dc23

LC record available at https://lccn.loc.gov/2021034701

LC ebook record available at https://lccn.loc.gov/2021034702

P 24 23 22 21 20 19 18 17 16 15 14 13 12 11 10 9 8 7 6 5 4 3 2 1

Y 41 40 39 38 37 36 35 34 33 32 31 30 29 28 27 26 25 24 23 22 21

CONTENTS

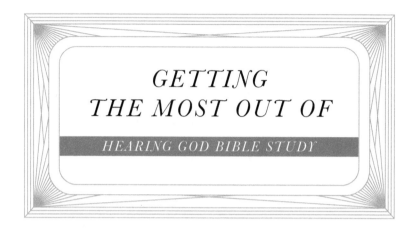

GETTING
THE MOST OUT OF

HEARING GOD BIBLE STUDY

KNOWING CHRIST is where faith begins. From there we are shaped through the essentials of discipleship: Bible study, prayer, Christian community, worship, and much more. We learn to grow in Christlike character, pursue justice, and share our faith with others. We persevere through doubts and gain wisdom for daily life. These are the topics woven into the IVP Signature Bible Studies. Working through this series will help you practice the essentials by exploring biblical truths found in classic books.

HOW IT'S PUT TOGETHER

Each session includes an opening quotation and suggested reading from the book *Hearing God*, a session goal to help guide your study, reflection questions to stir your thoughts on the topic, the text of the Bible passage, questions for exploring the passage, response questions to help you apply what you've learned, and a closing suggestion for prayer.

The workbook format is ideal for personal study and also allows group members to prepare in advance for discussions and record discussion notes. The responses you write here can form a permanent record of your thoughts and spiritual progress.

Throughout the guide are study-note sidebars that may be useful for group leaders or individuals. These notes do not give the answers, but they do provide additional background information on certain questions and can challenge participants to think deeper or differently about the content.

WHAT KIND OF GUIDE IS THIS?

The studies are not designed to merely tell you what one person thinks. Instead, through inductive study, they will help you discover for yourself what Scripture is saying. Each study deals with a particular passage—rather than jumping around the Bible—so that you can really delve into the biblical author's meaning in that context.

The studies ask three different kinds of questions about the Bible passage:

* *Observation* questions help you to understand the content of the passage by asking about the basic facts: who, what, when, where, and how.

* *Interpretation* questions delve into the meaning of the passage.

* *Application* questions help you discover implications for growing in Christ in your own life.

These three keys unlock the treasures of the biblical writings and help you live them out.

This is a thought-provoking guide. Each question assumes a variety of answers. Many questions do not have "right" answers, particularly questions that aim at meaning or application. Instead, the questions should inspire readers to explore the passage more thoroughly.

This study guide is flexible. You can use it for individual study, but it is also great for a variety of groups—student, professional, neighborhood, or church groups. Each study takes about forty-five minutes in a group setting or thirty minutes in personal study.

SUGGESTIONS FOR INDIVIDUAL STUDY

1. This guide is based on a classic book that will enrich your spiritual life. If you have not read *Hearing God,* you may want to read the portion recommended in the "Read" section before you begin your study. The ideas in the book will enhance your study, but the Bible text will be the focus of each session.

2. Begin each session with prayer, asking God to speak to you from his Word about this particular topic.

3. As you read the Scripture passage, reproduced for you from the New International Version, you may wish to mark phrases that seem important. Note in the margin any questions that come to your mind.

4. Close with the suggested prayer found at the end of each session. Speak to God about insights you have gained. Tell him of any desires you have for specific growth. Ask him to help you attempt to live out the principles described in that passage. You may wish to write your own prayer in this guide or a journal.

SUGGESTIONS FOR GROUP MEMBERS

Joining a Bible study group can be a great avenue to spiritual growth. Here are a few guidelines that will help you as you participate in the studies in this guide.

1. Reading the recommended portion of *Hearing God,* before or after each session, will enhance your study and understanding of the themes in this guide.

2. These studies use methods of inductive Bible study, which focuses on a particular passage of Scripture and works on it in depth. So try to dive into the given text instead of referring to other Scripture passages.

3. Questions are designed to help a group discuss together a passage of Scripture in order to understand its content, meaning, and implications. Most people are either natural talkers or natural listeners, yet this type of study works best if all members participate more or less evenly. Try to curb any natural tendency toward either excessive talking or excessive quiet. You and the rest of the group will benefit!

4. Most questions in this guide allow for a variety of answers. If you disagree with someone else's comment, gently say so. Then explain your own point of view from the passage before you.

5. Be willing to lead a discussion, if asked. Much of the preparation for leading has already been accomplished in the writing of this guide.

6. Respect the privacy of people in your group. Many people share things within the context of a Bible study group that they do not want to be public knowledge. Assume that personal information spoken within the group setting is private, unless you are specifically told otherwise.

7. We recommend that all groups agree on a few basic guidelines. You may wish to adapt this list to your situation:

   a. Anything said in this group is considered confidential and will not be discussed outside the group unless specific permission is given to do so.

   b. We will provide time for each person present to talk if he or she feels comfortable doing so.

    c. We will talk about ourselves and our own situations, avoiding conversation about other people.

    d. We will listen attentively to each other.

    e. We will pray for each other.

8. Enjoy your study. Prepare to grow!

SUGGESTIONS FOR GROUP LEADERS

There are specific suggestions to help you in the "Leading a Small Group" section. It describes how to lead a group discussion, gives helpful tips on group dynamics, and suggests ways to deal with problems that may arise during the discussion. With such help, someone with little or no experience can lead an effective group study. Read this section carefully, even if you are leading only one group meeting.

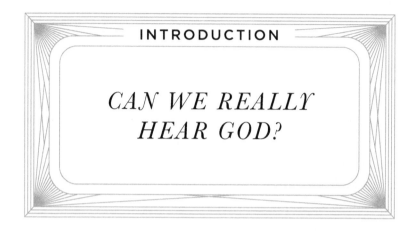

INTRODUCTION

CAN WE REALLY HEAR GOD?

HEARING GOD? A daring idea, some would say—presumptuous and even dangerous. But what if we are made for it? What if the human system simply will not function properly without it? There are good reasons to think it will not. The fine texture as well as the grand movements of life show our need to hear God. Isn't it more presumptuous and dangerous, in fact, to undertake human existence *without* hearing God?

We must think of ourselves as capable of having the same kinds of experiences as did Paul, Barnabas, or Elijah. They were people just like us, subject to like passions as we are (James 5:17). We must make the conscious effort to think that such things might happen to us and to imagine what it would be like if they were to happen. They are examples of the normal human life God intended for us: God's indwelling his people through personal presence and fellowship. Given our basic nature, we live— really live—only through God's regular speaking in our souls and thus "by every word that comes from of the mouth of God."

God has created us for intimate friendship with himself. Jesus told his followers that he and his Father would "come to them and make our home with them" (John 14:23). Certainly this abiding of the Son and the Father in the faithful heart involves conscious communication or conversation. The Spirit who inhabits us is not mute, restricting himself to an occasional nudge or a case of goosebumps. This is confirmed not only from Scripture but also by examples set by well-known Christians. Ideally we can be engaged in personal communion with God. We might well ask, "How could there be a personal relationship, a personal walk with God—or with anyone else—*without* individualized communication?"

Sometimes today it seems that our personal relationship with God is treated as no more than a mere arrangement or understanding that Jesus and his Father have about us. We have sinned, and Jesus has paid the "sin bill" for us. But shouldn't there be more to a personal relationship than that? A mere benefactor, however powerful, kind, and thoughtful, is not the same thing as a *friend*. Jesus says, "I have called you friends" (John 15:15) and "Look, I am with you every minute, even to the end of the age" (Matthew 28:20, paraphrase; see also Hebrews 13:5-6).

As our friend, God walks and talks in our midst as part of how the kingdom of God is in our midst (Luke 17:21). We are participants in the kingdom, not spectators. Accordingly, we seek to interact with God in a relationship of listening and speaking. Notice the interaction: "If my people, who are called by my name, will humble themselves and pray and *seek my face* and turn from their wicked ways, then *I will hear* from heaven, and I will forgive their sin and will heal their land" (2 Chronicles 7:14). If we humble ourselves and seek God, he will respond. Such interaction is part of our friendship with God.

CONVERSING WITH GOD

1 SAMUEL 16:1-13

THE LORD INTENDS FOR US to have a conversational relationship with him. In such a life, we learn to readily recognize his voice speaking in our hearts as occasion demands. God has made ample provision for this to happen in order to fulfill his mission as the Good Shepherd, which is to bring us life and life more abundantly. The abundance of life comes in following him, and "his sheep follow him because they know his voice" (John 10:4).

It is essential to the strength of our faith that we are in some measure capable of inwardly identifying with Samuel's experience in this passage, as he conversed with the Lord in the midst of Jesse's family. Such conversation makes life a partnership with God, open to new ideas and adventures.

SESSION GOAL	READ
Observe that God leads step by step as we converse with him about the things that matter to us.	Preface and chapter one of *Hearing God*

REFLECT

* Some people feel impatient to reach their destination, while others seem to patiently enjoy the journey—whether that be going to college or traveling. Where do you usually find yourself: eager to arrive, patient on the journey, unwilling to start, or somewhere else?

✳ When, if ever, have you wished God would just give you the answer? The verdict? Now?

STUDY

Following God's instruction, Samuel had anointed Saul to be king of all Israel. But as Saul turned from God and ignored God's instructions, God regretted having made Saul king. Samuel, the judge and prophet who had anointed Saul, was disappointed and angry and cried out to the Lord all that night (1 Samuel 15:11). *Read 1 Samuel 16:1-13.*

> ¹The LORD said to Samuel, "How long will you mourn for Saul, since I have rejected him as king over Israel? Fill your horn with oil and be on your way; I am sending you to Jesse of Bethlehem. I have chosen one of his sons to be king."
>
> ²But Samuel said, "How can I go? If Saul hears about it, he will kill me."
>
> The LORD said, "Take a heifer with you and say, 'I have come to sacrifice to the LORD.' ³Invite Jesse to the sacrifice, and I will show you what to do. You are to anoint for me the one I indicate."
>
> ⁴Samuel did what the LORD said. When he arrived at Bethlehem, the elders of the town trembled when they met him. They asked, "Do you come in peace?"

⁵Samuel replied, "Yes, in peace; I have come to sacrifice to the Lord. Consecrate yourselves and come to the sacrifice with me." Then he consecrated Jesse and his sons and invited them to the sacrifice.

⁶When they arrived, Samuel saw Eliab and thought, "Surely the Lord's anointed stands here before the Lord."

⁷But the Lord said to Samuel, "Do not consider his appearance or his height, for I have rejected him. The Lord does not look at the things people look at. People look at the outward appearance, but the Lord looks at the heart."

⁸Then Jesse called Abinadab and had him pass in front of Samuel. But Samuel said, "The Lord has not chosen this one either." ⁹Jesse then had Shammah pass by, but Samuel said, "Nor has the Lord chosen this one." ¹⁰Jesse had seven of his sons pass before Samuel, but Samuel said to him, "The Lord has not chosen these." ¹¹So he asked Jesse, "Are these all the sons you have?"

"There is still the youngest," Jesse answered. "He is tending the sheep."

Samuel said, "Send for him; we will not sit down until he arrives."

¹²So he sent for him and had him brought in. He was glowing with health and had a fine appearance and handsome features.

Then the Lord said, "Rise and anoint him; this is the one."

¹³So Samuel took the horn of oil and anointed him in the presence of his brothers, and from that day on the Spirit of the Lord came powerfully upon David. Samuel then went to Ramah.

1. Why was Samuel reluctant to go to Jesse's house? (See 1 Samuel 15:10-11; 16:1-2.)

2. Conversational life with God involves asking questions. What question did God ask Samuel? What question did Samuel ask God?

3. What does a person need to think, feel, or believe about God in order to unhesitatingly ask God questions?

4. What does it tell you about Samuel that he didn't insist on knowing the instructions before leaving home, but moved forward on God's assurance that he would show him what to do (v. 3)?

> The Bethlehem town elders questioned Samuel about coming in peace (v. 4). This could have been a simple question about whether this was an official visit of Samuel the judge-prophet, or if Samuel was acting as an emissary for the suspicious and vindictive King Saul (1 Samuel 7:15; 22:6-19).

5. What about Eliab apparently made Samuel think he might be the one God was choosing to be king?

> When Samuel anointed Saul, Israel's first king, the text says Saul was "as handsome a young man as could be found anywhere in Israel, and he was a head taller than anyone else" (1 Samuel 9:2). But Saul did not live up to expectations.

6. God answered Samuel's thought by saying he didn't look at someone the way people did. Today, what are the things people look at to consider someone a potential leader for God?

7. Taking into account the character of God and how God works with people, what do you think God was looking for in a king (v. 7)?

8. The choice of David seems to have been unexpected, possibly surprising Samuel, Jesse, and Jesse's other sons. What has to be true about us in order for us to expect the unexpected from God?

RESPOND

* What would you most like about having a conversational life with God?

* What are you and God doing together these days? If you're not sure, ask God right now to show you.

PRAY

As you pray, experiment with conversing with God about the ordinary events of your life. Ask God to help you grow in your awareness of his friendship and approach life as a conversation with him. Thank God for helping you learn to readily recognize his voice speaking in your heart.

NEXT STEPS

This week, pause briefly between everyday tasks, being open to anything God might want to say to you about these tasks. You might want to have a special object or picture nearby to help you pause and be still for a minute or two.

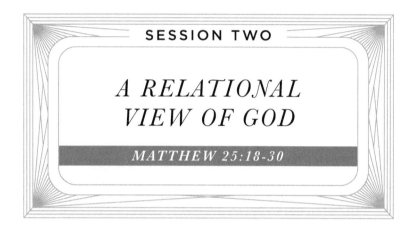

SESSION TWO

A RELATIONAL VIEW OF GOD

MATTHEW 25:18-30

FAR TOO COMMONLY, people think of God as did the one-talent servant in the parable of the talents who regarded his master as a harsh person. He was, accordingly, afraid of his master and gave him back exactly what "belonged" to him. Such a person could not "share [his] master's happiness" because—misconceiving their relationship as he did—he could neither enter into his master's mind and life nor open his own life to him. This third servant actually abused his master by taking him to be interested only in getting his own back, while the master for his part was really interested in sharing his life and goods with others.

SESSION GOAL	READ
Observe the need to understand God as a friend and coworker in order to have a conversational relationship.	Chapters two and three of *Hearing God*

⚹〰 REFLECT 〰

⁕ Why do people sometimes feel that God is disappointed in them?

✳ Who is someone you have known who seems to view God as generous and kind, loving yet firm?

——⫸ STUDY ⫷——

This is a parable Jesus tells about mutual trust between a master and his servants. In Matthew 25:14-17, the master trusts three servants with wealth, giving them five, two, and one bag(s) of gold, respectively. The first two servants, trusting that their master is fair and good, invest their gold. (The phrase *bags of gold* is used in the New International Version instead of the traditional word *talent*.) ***Read Matthew 25:18-30.***

> [18]"But the man who had received one bag [of gold] went off, dug a hole in the ground and hid his master's money.
>
> [19]"After a long time the master of those servants returned and settled accounts with them. [20]The man who had received five bags of gold brought the other five. 'Master,' he said, 'you entrusted me with five bags of gold. See, I have gained five more.'
>
> [21]"His master replied, 'Well done, good and faithful servant! You have been faithful with a few things; I will put you in charge of many things. Come and share your master's happiness!'
>
> [22]"The man with two bags of gold also came. 'Master,' he said, 'you entrusted me with two bags of gold; see, I have gained two more.'
>
> [23]"His master replied, 'Well done, good and faithful servant! You have been faithful with a few things; I will put you in charge of many things. Come and share your master's happiness!'

²⁴"Then the man who had received one bag of gold came. 'Master,' he said, 'I knew that you are a hard man, harvesting where you have not sown and gathering where you have not scattered seed. ²⁵So I was afraid and went out and hid your gold in the ground. See, here is what belongs to you.'

²⁶"His master replied, 'You wicked, lazy servant! So you knew that I harvest where I have not sown and gather where I have not scattered seed? ²⁷Well then, you should have put my money on deposit with the bankers, so that when I returned I would have received it back with interest.'

²⁸"'So take the bag of gold from him and give it to the one who has ten bags. ²⁹For whoever has will be given more, and they will have an abundance. Whoever does not have, even what they have will be taken from them. ³⁰And throw that worthless servant outside, into the darkness, where there will be weeping and gnashing of teeth.'"

1. How did the first and second servants exhibit trust in their master?

2. What contemporary words or phrases may be used to describe how the third servant viewed the master?

3. In what way did the third servant's view of his master affect his actions and hinder his capacity to share in the happiness of his master as the other servants did (vv. 21, 23)?

4. How might people's lack of practical trust in God create problems for them, such as fearing they might disappoint God?

> We demean God by casting him in the role of the taskmaster, cosmic boss, foreman, or autocrat, whose chief joy in relation to humans is ordering them around and painstakingly noting down any failures. Instead, we are to be God's friends (2 Chronicles 20:7; John 15:13-15) and fellow workers (1 Corinthians 3:9).

5. In what ways did the first and second servants become friends and fellow workers with the master?

6. In what way was the third servant himself hardhearted, which is what he presumed the master to be?

> The third servant resembles the hardhearted scribes and the Pharisees referred to earlier in this discourse (Matthew 23–25). Jesus had described them as "burying" the law and the temple in legalism and even extortion (23:13-36). Even though Jesus longed to care for them as a mother hen does, they would have none of it. When Rome later destroyed Jerusalem, their "house was left to you desolate" (23:37-38), accompanied by great suffering ("weeping and gnashing of teeth").*

7. The third servant is described as "wicked" (v. 26) in the sense of making false assumptions about God. In what ways do people today make false assumptions about God as the third servant did about his master (v. 24)?

"God is light; in him there is no darkness at all" (1 John 1:5). In other words, it's unwise to think *anything* bad about God. God's Trinitarian nature will always involve love, joy, peace, forbearance, kindness, goodness, faithfulness, gentleness, and self-control. Even when saying things that are difficult to hear, God speaks the truth in love (Galatians 5:22-23; Ephesians 4:15).

8. How do we share in God's happiness as God's friends and fellow workers?

 RESPOND

⁕ In what areas of life are you tempted to think that God is constantly disappointed in you?

✳ In what ways is God so much better than you think? More patient, kind, not rude or insisting everything go his way, not irritable or resentful (1 Corinthians 13:4-6, NRSV)?

 **PRAY**

As you pray, include the words and ideas from Psalm 103:1-13, remembering God's benefits of forgiveness, healing, redemption, love, and mercy. Focus especially on verse 10: "He does not treat us as our sins deserve or repay us according to our iniquities." Thank God for these things and ask for help in making them part of your experience of God.

 **NEXT STEPS**

This week ask God to show you if there are elements of task-master, cosmic boss, foreman, or autocrat in your view of him. Then journal or talk with someone you trust about your current view of God and how you would like for it to expand.

---

*See Tom Wright, *Matthew for Everyone* (London: SPCK Westminster/John Knox Press, 2014), 136-39.

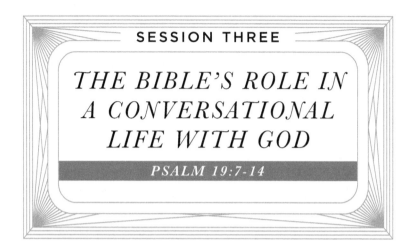

THE BIBLE'S ROLE IN A CONVERSATIONAL LIFE WITH GOD

PSALM 19:7-14

THE BIBLE EXPRESSES the mind of God, since God himself speaks to us through its pages. Thus, in understanding the Bible, we come to share God's thoughts and attitudes and even his life through his Word. Scripture is a *communication* that establishes *communion* and opens the way to *union*, all in a way that is perfectly understandable once we begin to have experience of it. The eager use of the Bible leads naturally and tangibly to the mind of God and the person of Christ.

The Bible has its own special and irreplaceable role in our life with God. God will meet any person who approaches it openly, honestly, intelligently, and persistently through its pages and will speak peace to their souls.

SESSION GOAL	READ
Consider the centrality of reading the Bible openly, honestly, intelligently, and persistently in developing a conversational life with God.	Chapters four, five, and six of *Hearing God*

REFLECT

* Why is reading Scripture very different from reading any other book?

* When, if ever, have you experienced times of meeting God while being immersed in Scripture (by reading or teaching)?

STUDY

In this passage, the words "law" or "statutes" or "commands of the LORD" (and so on) refer to the totality of what God says and who God is. You may wish to substitute those words with "whatever God says" or "loving God and others" (Matthew 22:36-40; Galatians 5:14). "Perfect" in this passage refers to wholeness and completeness for life. ***Read Psalm 19:7-14.***

> 7The law of the LORD is perfect,
>   refreshing the soul.
> The statutes of the LORD are trustworthy,
>   making wise the simple.
> 8The precepts of the LORD are right,
>   giving joy to the heart.
> The commands of the LORD are radiant,
>   giving light to the eyes.
> 9The fear of the LORD is pure,
>   enduring forever.
> The decrees of the LORD are firm,
>   and all of them are righteous.

¹⁰They are more precious than gold,
    than much pure gold;
they are sweeter than honey,
    than honey from the honeycomb.
¹¹By them your servant is warned;
    in keeping them there is great reward.
¹²But who can discern their own errors?
    Forgive my hidden faults.
¹³Keep your servant also from willful sins;
    may they not rule over me.
Then I will be blameless,
    innocent of great transgression.

¹⁴May these words of my mouth and this meditation of
        my heart
    be pleasing in your sight,
    Lord, my Rock and my Redeemer.

1. What characteristics of Scripture do you find in this passage?

2. Which of these characteristics is most practical to our culture today?

"Fear of the Lord" is not about having feelings of terror, but of having an appropriate, rightly deserved, and intense awe and respect for God.

3. What other phrases besides "fear of the LORD" indicate an element of worship by the psalmist?

4. What did the psalmist request in prayer (vv. 11-14)?

> Notice the shift in verse 11 from speaking *about Scripture* to speaking directly *to God*. Reading the Bible works best in combination with prayer so that the words flow from God; it creates living conversation. And study is best accompanied by worship because knowledge of God and his ways leaves the reader reverent and amazed.

5. How does confession flow organically from viewing God's greatness in the revelation of Scripture (vv. 12-13)?

> Meditating on the wonders of the law and God's greatness in general seems to have created a longing for deep transformation in the psalmist (vv. 12-13).

6. Why might it be important to address hidden faults as well as obvious willful ones (vv. 12-13)?

7. What contemporary words might be used along with "Rock" and "Redeemer" to indicate God's dependability and willingness to bring us out of darkness into light?

> The Scriptures are an amazing treasure, but people can use the Bible to support their personal position. When they come to the Scriptures with an open heart, they will see the Word light up. The test is: Is this serving what I want or what God wants? When living in a conversational relationship with God, we have to let go of our efforts to manipulate him or others. We must receive the word that comes from him through the Scriptures. William Law comments, "Therefore the Scriptures should only be read in an attitude of prayer, trusting to the inward working of the Holy Spirit to make their truths a living reality within us."*

 **RESPOND**

✳ Look at the opening paragraphs of this session and the paragraph above. What phrases help you remember that reading Scripture is about meeting with God in conversation?

✳ What approaches or styles of Bible reading best create a
space for you to meet God in Scripture?

 PRAY

Thank God for his eagerness to "refresh the soul," "give joy to
the heart," and any other phrase from Psalm 19. Continue by
praying verses 11-14, pausing and saying them slowly so that you
are praying the words and ideas.

 NEXT STEPS

This week, preface times of Bible reading with the phrases you
have underlined in this session to remind you that you are
meeting with God and setting yourself up for conversation all
day long with God.

---

*William Law, *The Power of the Spirit: Selections from the Writings of William Law,* ed. Dave
Hunt (Fort Washington, PA: Christian Literature Crusade, 1971), 62.

THE STILL, SMALL VOICE

1 KINGS 19:2-18

GOD ADDRESSES US IN VARIOUS WAYS: in dreams, visions, and voices; through the Bible and extraordinary events. Yet the still small voice—the interior or inner voice, as it is also called—is the preferred and most valuable form of individual communication for God's purposes. God usually addresses individually those who walk with him in a mature, personal relationship using this inner voice, showing forth the reality of the kingdom of God as they go.

The primary subjective way that God addresses us is our own spirits—our own thoughts and feelings toward ourselves as well as toward events and people around us. This mode is best suited to the redemptive purposes of God because *it most engages the faculties of free, intelligent beings involved in the work of God as his colaborers and friends.*

SESSION GOAL	READ
Understand that God speaks primarily in the still, small voice in a conversational relationship with humans.	Chapter seven of *Hearing God*

✳ How do we usually respond to someone who speaks quietly to us?

✳ If God were to speak to you, what form would be the easiest for you to hear? A loud voice, a conversational tone, a whisper?

STUDY

The powerful prophet Elijah had just won a contest with the prophets of the false god Baal. Elijah called down fire from heaven on his sacrifice, but Baal did not respond at all to his prophets. The prophets of Baal were conquered, but this made their chief advocate, Jezebel the queen of Israel, very angry with Elijah. *Read 1 Kings 19:2-18.*

> ²So Jezebel sent a messenger to Elijah to say, "May the gods deal with me, be it ever so severely, if by this time tomorrow I do not make your life like that of one of them."
>
> ³Elijah was afraid and ran for his life. When he came to Beersheba in Judah, he left his servant there, ⁴while he himself went a day's journey into the wilderness. He came to a broom bush, sat down under it and prayed that he might die. "I have had enough, Lord," he said. "Take my life; I am no better than my ancestors." ⁵Then he lay down under the bush and fell asleep.

All at once an angel touched him and said, "Get up and eat." ⁶He looked around, and there by his head was some bread baked over hot coals, and a jar of water. He ate and drank and then lay down again.

⁷The angel of the LORD came back a second time and touched him and said, "Get up and eat, for the journey is too much for you." ⁸So he got up and ate and drank. Strengthened by that food, he traveled forty days and forty nights until he reached Horeb, the mountain of God. ⁹There he went into a cave and spent the night.

And the word of the LORD came to him: "What are you doing here, Elijah?"

¹⁰He replied, "I have been very zealous for the LORD God Almighty. The Israelites have rejected your covenant, torn down your altars, and put your prophets to death with the sword. I am the only one left, and now they are trying to kill me too."

¹¹The LORD said, "Go out and stand on the mountain in the presence of the LORD, for the LORD is about to pass by."

Then a great and powerful wind tore the mountains apart and shattered the rocks before the LORD, but the LORD was not in the wind. After the wind there was an earthquake, but the LORD was not in the earthquake. ¹²After the earthquake came a fire, but the LORD was not in the fire. And after the fire came a gentle whisper. ¹³When Elijah heard it, he pulled his cloak over his face and went out and stood at the mouth of the cave.

Then a voice said to him, "What are you doing here, Elijah?"

¹⁴He replied, "I have been very zealous for the LORD God Almighty. The Israelites have rejected your covenant, torn down your altars, and put your prophets to death with

the sword. I am the only one left, and now they are trying to kill me too."

¹⁵The LORD said to him, "Go back the way you came, and go to the Desert of Damascus. When you get there, anoint Hazael king over Aram. ¹⁶Also, anoint Jehu son of Nimshi king over Israel, and anoint Elisha son of Shaphat from Abel Meholah to succeed you as prophet. ¹⁷Jehu will put to death any who escape the sword of Hazael, and Elisha will put to death any who escape the sword of Jehu. ¹⁸Yet I reserve seven thousand in Israel—all whose knees have not bowed down to Baal and whose mouths have not kissed him."

1. How did Elijah respond to Jezebel's death threat?

Elijah would have run about ninety miles from the north of Judea to the southern edge. The wilderness he traveled was stark, barren country, and the tall, bushy tree would have been a welcome sight. Then the journey to Mount Horeb was two to three hundred miles depending on the route.

2. How did the angel help Elijah?

3. How did God approach Elijah in conversation (v. 9)?

4. How did God choose to respond to Elijah's desire to die (vv. 4-5)? How do you respond?

Many speculate that Elijah was hoping to replicate Moses' dramatic experience at Mount Horeb (Mount Sinai). This was where Moses received the Ten Commandments in a display of thunder, lightning, fire, smoke, quaking earth, and a trumpet blast (Exodus 19:16-19). Also, God placed Moses in "a cleft in a rock," covering him with his "hand" as his "goodness" passed in front of him (Exodus 33:21-22).

5. How did Elijah's experience compare with Moses' experience (vv. 9-13)?

6. What elements of conversation did Elijah experience with God?

"A still, small voice" (KJV) is translated in several ways, including "a gentle whisper" (v. 12). Each expression places the emphasis on the inconspicuous or unassuming way the message came.

7. Why might some people prefer dreams, visions, voices, or appearances of angels? Why might others prefer the still, small voice?

8. What next steps did God give Elijah, and how might they have encouraged him (vv. 15-18)?

9. What can we learn about how God interacts with people in conversation from this close-up of Elijah's conversation with God?

⁕ RESPOND ⁕

※ Which of Elijah's actions might assist you in having conversations with God: asking God questions, stating true feelings (that others would deem unacceptable), going to a place that helps you connect with God, or something else you noticed?

✳ What questions (no matter how seemingly faithless) would you like to ask God, or what requests would you like to make, as Elijah did?

PRAY

Ask God to guide you in engaging him in conversations about your real life. Thank God for accepting you and being eager to hear you and give you next steps.

NEXT STEPS

This week when you have feelings that some might think are inappropriate for a Christian, take time to lay them out honestly before God. Be open to needing some rest and good food (as the angel provided for Elijah). Also be open to whatever way God chooses to meet you.

LISTENING FOR GOD

When I want to hear from God, I ask him to speak to me. Then as I go through my days, I listen for the voice or the thought that comes from him to help me understand things. When we do ask in this way, we expect it and watch for it. I'm often in the midst of something else when the answer comes.

After I ask for God to speak to me, I find it works best if I devote the next hour or so to some kind of activity that neither engrosses my attention with other things nor allows me to be intensely focused on the matter in question. Housework, gardening, driving about on errands, or paying bills will generally do. I have learned not to worry about whether or not this is going to work. I know that it does not *have* to work, but I am sure that it *will* work if God has something he really wants me to know or do. This is, ultimately, because *I am sure of how great and good he is.*

Often by the end of an hour or so there has stood forth within my consciousness an idea or thought with that peculiar quality, spirit, and content that I have come to associate with God's voice. If so, I may write it down for further study. I may also decide to discuss the matter with others, usually without informing them that "God has told me. . . ." Or I may decide to reconsider the matter by repeating the same process after a short period of time. If you are uncertain if this is from you or from God, ask for further confirmation as Gideon did (Judges 6:11-40). You might say, "Please speak to me again" or "Lord, would you make that clearer?" That is the natural way we would relate to another person. We ask for clarity. I usually put a limit of two to three days on it.

Being uncertain doesn't mean you haven't heard. Remember too that scientists check their results by re-running experiments. We should be so humble.

If, on the other hand, nothing emerges by the end of an hour or so, I am not alarmed. I set myself to hold the matter before God as I go about my business and confidently get on with my life. Of course I make it a point to *keep* listening. Very often, within a day something happens through which God's voice, recognizably distinct, is heard.

If I am given nothing, my next step is to ask God, "Is there anything in me that is preventing you from speaking clearly about this matter? If there is something in my attitude, please tell me." That answer may come in various ways. I don't believe God messes with our minds. He is not mean, and if he has something to say to me, he will say it.

If this does not happen, I generally cease to seek God's word specifically on the matter in question. I do not cease my *general* attitude of listening. But I am neither disappointed nor alarmed, nor even concerned. I do as seems best.

(Adapted from *Hearing God*, 261-62)

HEARING THE UNEXPECTED

ACTS 10:9-23, 44-48

GOD OFTEN SPEAKS *without* our seeking his individualized word to us. Gimmicks and methods do not make this happen. But God's speaking comes easily to those with a life surrendered to God—those who have a humble openness to his direction even when it is contrary to our wants and assumptions. As we become experienced with the way his word comes to us, we learn to offer fervent but patient requests for guidance.

SESSION GOAL	READ
Recognize that God may say unexpected things and ask us to interact with unfamiliar people.	Chapter eight of *Hearing God*

 REFLECT

❋ Peter is generally regarded as being open to new experiences (like walking on water!). Are you more like adventurous Peter, more eager to stay in a familiar setting, or somewhere in the middle?

☀ How does God generally seem to get your attention—through others' words, Bible verses, strong emotions, or some other way?

STUDY

Prior to this passage, an angel of God appeared to the Roman centurion, Cornelius, who was "devout and God-fearing." The angel told Cornelius to send for Peter, who was staying thirty miles away in Joppa (Acts 10:1-8). Cornelius did as the angel instructed. In the meantime Peter also heard from God. ***Read Acts 10:9-23, 44-48.***

> [9]About noon the following day as they [Cornelius's servants] were on their journey and approaching the city, Peter went up on the roof to pray. [10]He became hungry and wanted something to eat, and while the meal was being prepared, he fell into a trance. [11]He saw heaven opened and something like a large sheet being let down to earth by its four corners. [12]It contained all kinds of four-footed animals, as well as reptiles and birds. [13]Then a voice told him, "Get up, Peter. Kill and eat."
>
> [14]"Surely not, Lord!" Peter replied. "I have never eaten anything impure or unclean."
>
> [15]The voice spoke to him a second time, "Do not call anything impure that God has made clean."
>
> [16]This happened three times, and immediately the sheet was taken back to heaven.
>
> [17]While Peter was wondering about the meaning of the vision, the men sent by Cornelius found out where Simon's

house was and stopped at the gate. [18]They called out, asking if Simon who was known as Peter was staying there.

[19]While Peter was still thinking about the vision, the Spirit said to him, "Simon, three men are looking for you. [20]So get up and go downstairs. Do not hesitate to go with them, for I have sent them."

[21]Peter went down and said to the men, "I'm the one you're looking for. Why have you come?"

[22]The men replied, "We have come from Cornelius the centurion. He is a righteous and God-fearing man, who is respected by all the Jewish people. A holy angel told him to ask you to come to his house so that he could hear what you have to say." [23]Then Peter invited the men into the house to be his guests. The next day Peter started out with them, and some of the believers from Joppa went along. . . .

[44]While Peter was still speaking these words, the Holy Spirit came on all who heard the message. [45]The circumcised believers who had come with Peter were astonished that the gift of the Holy Spirit had been poured out even on Gentiles. [46]For they heard them speaking in tongues and praising God.

Then Peter said, [47]"Surely no one can stand in the way of their being baptized with water. They have received the Holy Spirit just as we have." [48]So he ordered that they be baptized in the name of Jesus Christ. Then they asked Peter to stay with them for a few days.

1. What was Peter doing when he "fell into a trance"?

2. How would you describe Peter's experience in verses 9-13?

3. Describe the conversation between the "voice" and Peter, especially anything that surprises you.

> Peter is appropriately shocked by this vision because the Mosaic law prohibited the eating of several kinds of meat (Leviticus 11). Jewish leaders had imposed even more restrictions as time had passed.

4. What might have been Peter's feelings as he exclaimed, "I have never eaten anything impure or unclean"?

5. Why might the repetition of the vision three times have helped Peter?

6. How did the Spirit come alongside Peter and give him a next step (vv. 19-23)?

> It's unusual for Peter to invite the servants of a Gentile into the house to be his guests. Even more striking is Peter's acceptance of an invitation from a powerful military officer, which may have required courage and confidence. Peter seems to have been gradually absorbing God's idea that the kingdom of God would now include Gentiles as well as Jews.

7. Peter's response to the Spirit's witness was quite forceful. What words of his sent a message that this occurrence was indeed from God and not to be doubted (vv. 47-48)?

8. In this passage, how did Peter follow God's leading step by step without knowing where it would lead?

> Peter followed God's leading in ushering in the "mystery of his will according to his good pleasure, which he purposed in Christ, to be put into effect when the times reach their fulfillment—to bring unity to all things in heaven and on earth under Christ" (Ephesians 1:9-10). But this inclusion of the Gentiles in the kingdom of God must have seemed to Peter to have gone against everything he had learned. No doubt his experience in receiving "instructions through the Holy Spirit" (Acts 1:2) had led him so well, that he was willing to hear the most unexpected instructions and fellowship with people he had disregarded his entire life.

RESPOND

✳ How open are you to hearing something unexpected—out of your tradition—from God?

✳ If God were to lead you step by step into a new—perhaps intimidating—experience, what might you do to move from fear and doubt to courage and confidence?

PRAY

As you pray, express trust in the Lord. Thank him for offering you step-by-step directions into new adventures. Ask God to give you a willing spirit to do so.

NEXT STEPS

This week listen attentively during your Bible reading and interactions with people for invitations to welcome others you may be a bit uncomfortable with. Be willing to converse with God if you experience hesitation and doubts, knowing God is patient, as he was with Peter (and not unwilling to tell you something three times!).

COLABORERS WITH GOD

1 CHRONICLES 14:8-17

HEARING GOD IS A CONVERSATION THAT involves prayer. Prayer is an honest exchange between people who are doing things together. As you and God work together, you need to invoke his power in that activity. Joint activity is a key to understanding how conversation flows. We understand what God is doing so well that we often know exactly what he is thinking and intending to do.

Because we are God's colaborers, our wants and desires are also important to God and God's plan for us (1 Corinthians 3:9). His intent for us is that we would grow to the point where we would do what we want because what we want is part of that shared understanding with God, our friend.

SESSION GOAL	**READ**
Observe how colaborers with God freely engage in conversation with God.	Chapter nine and epilogue of *Hearing God*

* If we think of prayer as an honest exchange between people who are doing things together, what have you and God been doing together lately?

* Who is someone you know who seems to work closely with God, knowing what to say and do but not making it about themselves?

STUDY

David experienced working together with God in close relationship. ***Read 1 Chronicles 14:8-17.***

⁸When the Philistines heard that David had been anointed king over all Israel, they went up in full force to search for him, but David heard about it and went out to meet them. ⁹Now the Philistines had come and raided the Valley of Rephaim; ¹⁰so David inquired of God: "Shall I go and attack the Philistines? Will you deliver them into my hands?"

The LORD answered him, "Go, I will deliver them into your hands."

¹¹So David and his men went up to Baal Perazim, and there he defeated them. He said, "As waters break out, God has broken out against my enemies by my hand." So that place was called Baal Perazim. ¹²The Philistines had

abandoned their gods there, and David gave orders to burn them in the fire.

¹³Once more the Philistines raided the valley; ¹⁴so David inquired of God again, and God answered him, "Do not go directly after them, but circle around them and attack them in front of the poplar trees. ¹⁵As soon as you hear the sound of marching in the tops of the poplar trees, move out to battle, because that will mean God has gone out in front of you to strike the Philistine army." ¹⁶So David did as God commanded him, and they struck down the Philistine army, all the way from Gibeon to Gezer.

¹⁷So David's fame spread throughout every land, and the LORD made all the nations fear him.

1. The average military leader who experiences an enemy attacking and raiding his people would probably automatically plan a counterattack. What did David do (v. 10)?

2. How did the Philistines unknowingly benefit from their first defeat by the Israelites (v. 12)?

3. Focus on these words in verse 14: "David inquired of God again." In what ways was this possibly an unusual thing for a military leader-king to do?

4. David asked God questions about important circumstances, unlike prayers that devolve into pleading with God to do what we want. What are the benefits of asking God questions instead?

5. How did David respond to God's unusual battle plan?

6. Try to picture what it was like for Israelite soldiers to stand waiting for the sound of God marching in the tops of the poplar trees, and then charge forward. How might those soldiers have felt?

> Saints who have been drawn into friendship and single-focused service with God become something no one has ever seen before. They grow as individuals who are increasingly unique because God has shaped their hearts and their wills (Proverbs 3:5-6). Their desires match up with God's desires and they are empowered to do things that both God and they want.

7. What are good questions we might ask God regarding upcoming meetings or luncheons or family gatherings?

> God gives us as his colaborers the power of
> creativity, and we delight in our creativity. That
> shared understanding and creative activity results in
> circumstances and relationships far beyond our power
> or anything we could imagine. We are moving toward
> having the "mind of Christ" (1 Corinthians 2:16).

8. How did David's habit of asking God questions make him a
   like-minded partner for God to colabor with?

RESPOND

✳ For what situations might you ask God, What do I need to
   know about . . . ?

✳ What would you like about having the "mind of Christ" in
   general or in a specific situation?

PRAY

As you pray, ask God some questions. You may even want to ask God what you need to ask him about! You might ask about circumstances, relationships, health issues, finances: What do I need to know? Or, What is my next step?

NEXT STEPS

This week, make a conscious effort to pause and ask God questions as you start a new task or project, or as you approach someone who seems to be struggling or looking for attention.

LEADING A SMALL GROUP

LEADING A BIBLE DISCUSSION can be an enjoyable and rewarding experience. But it can also be intimidating—especially if you've never done it before. If this is how you feel, you're in good company.

Remember when God asked Moses to lead the Israelites out of Egypt? Moses replied, "Please send someone else" (Exodus 4:13)! But God gave Moses the help (human and divine) he needed to be a strong leader.

Leading a Bible discussion is not difficult if you follow certain guidelines. You don't need to be an expert on the Bible or a trained teacher. The suggestions listed below can help you to effectively fulfill your role as leader—and enjoy doing it.

PREPARING FOR THE STUDY

1. As you study the passage before the group meeting, ask God to help you understand it and apply it in your own life. Unless this happens, you will not be prepared to lead others. Pray too for the various members of the group. Ask God to open your hearts to the message of his Word and motivate you to action.

2. Read the introduction to the entire guide to get an overview of the subject at hand and the issues that will be explored.

3. Be ready to respond to the "Reflect" questions with a personal story or example. The group will be only as vulnerable and open as its leader.

4. Read the chapter of the companion book that is recommended at the beginning of the session.

5. Read and reread the assigned Bible passage to familiarize yourself with it. You may want to look up the passage in a Bible so that you can see its context.

6. This study guide is based on the New International Version of the Bible. It will help you and the group if you use this translation as the basis for your study and discussion.

7. Carefully work through each question in the study. Spend time in meditation and reflection as you consider how to respond.

8. Write your thoughts and responses in the space provided in the study guide. This will help you to express your understanding of the passage clearly.

9. It might help you to have a Bible dictionary handy. Use it to look up any unfamiliar words, names, or places.

10. Take the final (application) study questions and the "Respond" portion of each study seriously. Consider what this means for your life, what changes you may need to make in your lifestyle, or what actions you can take in your church or with people you know. Remember that the group will follow your lead in responding to the studies.

LEADING THE STUDY

1. Be sure everyone in your group has a study guide and a Bible. Encourage the group to prepare beforehand for each discussion by reading the introduction to the guide and by working through the questions for that session.

2. At the beginning of your first time together, explain that these studies are meant to be discussions, not lectures. Encourage the members of the group to participate. However, do not put pressure on those who may be hesitant to speak during the first few sessions.

3. Begin the study on time. Open with prayer, asking God to help the group understand and apply the passage.

4. Have a group member read aloud the introductory paragraph at the beginning of the discussion. This will remind the group of the topic of the study.

5. Discuss the "Reflect" questions before reading the Bible passage. These kinds of opening questions are important for several reasons. First, there is usually a stiffness that needs to be overcome before people will begin to talk openly. A good question will break the ice.

   Second, most people will have lots of different things going on in their minds (dinner, an exam, an important meeting coming up, how to get the car fixed) that have nothing to do with the study. A creative question will get their attention and draw them into the discussion.

   Third, opening questions can reveal where our thoughts or feelings need to be transformed by Scripture. That is why it is important not to read the passage before the "Reflect" questions are asked. The passage will tend to color the honest reactions people would otherwise give because they feel they are supposed to think the way the Bible does.

6. Have a group member read aloud the Scripture passage.

7. As you ask the questions, keep in mind that they are designed to be used just as they are written. You may simply read them aloud. Or you may prefer to express them in your own words.

   There may be times when it is appropriate to deviate from the study guide. For example, a question may already have been answered. If so, move on to the next question. Or someone may raise an important question not covered in the guide. Take time to discuss it, but try to keep the group from going off on tangents.

8. Avoid offering the first answer to a study question. Repeat or rephrase questions if necessary until they are clearly understood. An eager group quickly becomes passive and silent if members think the leader will give all the *right* answers.

9. Don't be afraid of silence. People may need time to think about the question before formulating their answers.

10. Don't be content with just one answer. Ask, "What do the rest of you think?" or, "Anything else?" until several people have given answers to a question. You might point out one of the study sidebars to help spur discussion; for example, "Does the quotation on page seventeen provide any insight as you think about this question?"

11. Acknowledge all contributions. Be affirming whenever possible. Never reject an answer. If it is clearly off base, ask, "Which verse led you to that conclusion?" or, "What do the rest of you think?"

12. Don't expect every answer to be addressed to you, even though this will probably happen at first. As group members become more at ease, they will begin to truly interact with each other. This is one sign of healthy discussion.

13. Don't be afraid of controversy. It can be stimulating! If you don't resolve an issue completely, don't be frustrated. Move on and keep it in mind for later. A subsequent study may solve the problem.

14. Try to periodically summarize what the group has said about the passage. This helps to draw together the various ideas mentioned and gives continuity to the study. But don't preach.

15. When you come to the application questions at the end of each "Study" section, be willing to keep the discussion going by describing how you have been affected by the study. It's important that we each apply the message of the passage to ourselves in a specific way.

    Depending on the makeup of your group and the length of time you've been together, you may or may not want to discuss the "Respond" section. If not, allow the group to read it and reflect on it silently. Encourage members to make specific commitments and to write them in their study guide. Ask them the following week how they did with their commitments.

16. Conclude your time together with conversational prayer. Ask for God's help in following through on the commitments you've made.

17. End the group discussion on time.

Many more suggestions and helps are found in The Big Book on Small Groups *by Jeffrey Arnold.*

SUGGESTED RESOURCES

Joyce Huggett, *The Joy of Listening to God: Hearing the Many Ways God Speaks to Us*

Joyce Huggett, *Listening to God*

Jan Johnson, *When the Soul Listens: Finding Rest and Direction in Contemplative Prayer*

Peter Lord, *Hearing God: An Easy-to-Follow, Step-by-Step Guide to Two-Way Communication with God*

Priscilla Shirer, *Discerning the Voice of God: How to Recognize When God Is Speaking*

Dallas Willard, *Hearing God Through the Year: A 365-Day Devotional*

THE IVP SIGNATURE COLLECTION

Since 1947 InterVarsity Press has been publishing thoughtful Christian books that serve the university, the church, and the world. In celebration of our seventy-fifth anniversary, IVP is releasing special editions of select iconic and bestselling books from throughout our history.

RELEASED IN 2019

Basic Christianity (1958)
JOHN STOTT

How to Give Away Your Faith (1966)
PAUL E. LITTLE

RELEASED IN 2020

The God Who Is There (1968)
FRANCIS A. SCHAEFFER

This Morning with God (1968)
EDITED BY CAROL ADENEY AND BILL WEIMER

The Fight (1976)
JOHN WHITE

Free at Last? (1983)
CARL F. ELLIS JR.

The Dust of Death (1973)
OS GUINNESS

The Singer (1975)
CALVIN MILLER

RELEASED IN 2021

Knowing God (1973)
J. I. PACKER

Out of the Saltshaker and Into the World
(1979) REBECCA MANLEY PIPPERT

A Long Obedience in the Same Direction
(1980) EUGENE H. PETERSON

More Than Equals (1993)
SPENCER PERKINS AND CHRIS RICE

Between Heaven and Hell (1982)
PETER KREEFT

Good News About Injustice (1999)
GARY A. HAUGEN

The Challenge of Jesus (1999)
N. T. WRIGHT

RELEASING IN 2022

Hearing God (1999)
DALLAS WILLARD

The Heart of Racial Justice (2004)
BRENDA SALTER McNEIL AND
RICK RICHARDSON

Sacred Rhythms (2006)
RUTH HALEY BARTON

Habits of the Mind (2000)
JAMES W. SIRE

True Story (2008)
JAMES CHOUNG

Scribbling in the Sand (2002)
MICHAEL CARD

The Next Worship (2015)
SANDRA MARIA VAN OPSTAL

Delighting in the Trinity (2012)
MICHAEL REEVES

Strong and Weak (2016)
ANDY CROUCH

Liturgy of the Ordinary (2016)
TISH HARRISON WARREN

IVP SIGNATURE BIBLE STUDIES

As companions to the IVP Signature Collection, IVP Signature Bible Studies feature the inductive study method, equipping individuals and groups to explore the biblical truths embedded in these books.

Basic Christianity Bible Study
JOHN STOTT

How to Give Away Your Faith Bible Study
PAUL E. LITTLE

The Singer Bible Study, CALVIN MILLER

Knowing God Bible Study, J. I. PACKER

A Long Obedience in the Same Direction Bible Study, EUGENE H. PETERSON

Good News About Injustice Bible Study
GARY A. HAUGEN

Hearing God Bible Study
DALLAS WILLARD

The Heart of Racial Justice Bible Study
BRENDA SALTER McNEIL AND
RICK RICHARDSON

True Story Bible Study, JAMES CHOUNG

The Next Worship Bible Study
SANDRA MARIA VAN OPSTAL

Strong and Weak Bible Study
ANDY CROUCH